MAINE

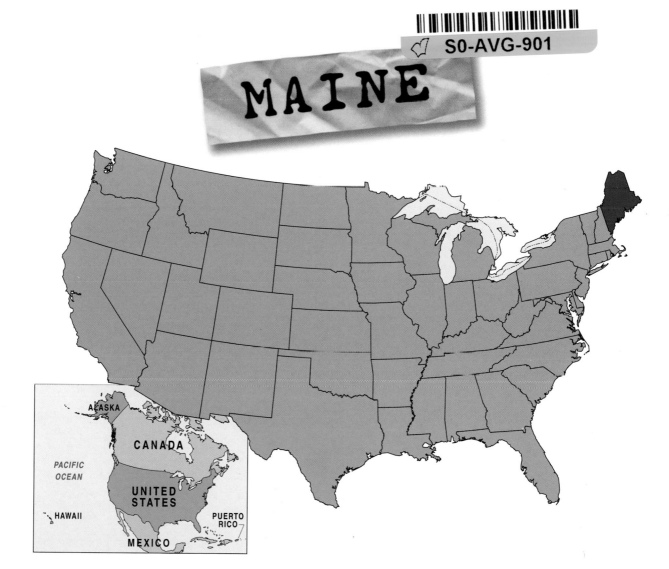

MAINE

HELLO
U.S.A.

by LeeAnne Engfer

Lerner Publications Company

You'll find this picture of Maine blueberries on the first page of every chapter. Blueberries grow in the wild and on farms in many parts of Maine. In fact, Maine is one of the biggest producers of blueberries in the United States. Sixty-three million pounds of blueberries are grown there every year!

Cover (left): Autumn in Acadia National Park. Cover (right): Lobster fishers near Swans Island. Pages 2-3: A water slide in Old Orchard Beach. Page 3: A moose cow near Rockwood.

This book is available in two editions:
Library binding by Lerner Publications Company, a division of Lerner Publishing Group
Soft cover by First Avenue Editions, an imprint of Lerner Publishing Group
241 First Avenue North
Minneapolis, MN 55401 U.S.A.

Website address: www.lernerbooks.com

LIBRARY OF CONGRESS CATALOGING-IN-PUBLICATION DATA

Engfer, LeeAnne, 1963–
    Maine / by LeeAnne Engfer (Revised and expanded 2nd edition)
      p. cm. — (Hello U.S.A.)
    Includes index.
    ISBN 0-8225-4071-1 (lib. bdg.: alk paper)
    ISBN 0-8225-4138-6 (pbk.: alk paper)
    1. Maine—Juvenile literature. [1. Maine.] I. Title. II. Series.
F19.3.E54 2002
974.1—dc21   2001001162

Manufactured in the United States of America
1 2 3 4 5 6 – JR – 07 06 05 04 03 02

CONTENTS

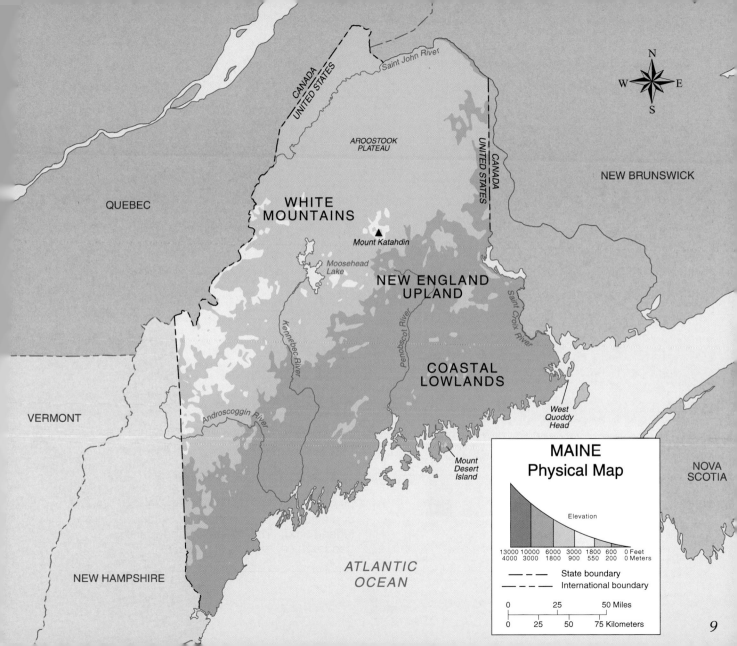

CANADA
UNITED STATES

Saint John River

QUEBEC

AROOSTOOK
PLATEAU

UNITED STATES
CANADA

NEW BRUNSWICK

WHITE
MOUNTAINS

▲
Mount Katahdin

Moosehead
Lake

NEW ENGLAND
UPLAND

Saint Croix River

Kennebec River

Penobscot River

COASTAL
LOWLANDS

Androscoggin River

West
Quoddy
Head

VERMONT

Mount
Desert
Island

NOVA
SCOTIA

NEW HAMPSHIRE

ATLANTIC
OCEAN

MAINE
Physical Map

Elevation

| 13000 | 10000 | 6000 | 3000 | 1800 | 600 | 0 Feet |
| 4000 | 3000 | 1800 | 900 | 550 | 200 | 0 Meters |

– – – State boundary

– – – International boundary

| 0 | 25 | 50 Miles |

| 0 | 25 | 50 | 75 Kilometers |

Beautiful landscapes, such as this peaceful pond, can be found on Mount Desert Island.

During the last **Ice Age,** which began about 80,000 years ago, sheets of ice up to a mile thick covered much of North America. By about 12,000 years ago, these **glaciers** had melted. The slow-moving ice ground down the Coastal Lowlands in southern Maine. The state's two other regions—the New England Upland and the White Mountains—are still hilly.

Melting ice from the glaciers created many lakes throughout the state and caused the sea level to rise. The rising ocean drowned hundreds of mountains and hills. Their peaks now form Maine's islands—there are about 2,000 of them. The largest is Mount Desert Island.

The Coastal Lowlands hug the shoreline along the Atlantic Ocean. The lowlands extend from 10 to 40 miles inland. Maine's coast twists and turns into

Maine's sandy beaches provide many opportunities for fun in the sun.

many bays. Miles of sandy beaches stretch along the southern shores. Farther north, huge rocks jut into the sea.

Mainers call the northeastern part of the coast "Down East," and many people refer to the state itself as Down East. Sailors first used the term in the 1800s when their ships were carried east from Boston toward Maine and Canada.

Cutting a band through the middle of the state, the New England Upland region rises from sea level in the east to nearly 2,000 feet in the southwest. In the northeastern part of this region lies the Aroostook Plateau—a flat highland with deep, fertile soil.

Many crops grow in the rich, fertile soil of the Aroostook Plateau.

The White Mountains stretch across northwestern Maine. Mount Katahdin, the highest point in the state, reaches nearly a mile into the sky.

Waterways abound in Maine. There are more than 5,000 lakes and ponds. Moosehead Lake is the largest. At least 5,000 rivers and streams run through the state. The longest rivers include the Saint John, Penobscot, Kennebec, and Androscoggin.

The names of many geographical features in Maine come from Native American words. The name *Androscoggin*, for example, means "place where fish are cured." *Katahdin* means "principal mountain."

The highest point in Maine is Mount Katahdin.

Vivid flowers such as the purple lupine *(left)* and lush green forests *(below)* add to Maine's natural colors.

Maine is home for many different types of wildlife, such as this white-tailed deer.

Woodlands cover almost 80 percent of Maine. Hunters, campers, and hikers have been known to get lost in the far-reaching woods. In northern and eastern Maine, spruce, fir, and white pine trees are common. In the south and central regions, birch, beech, maple, and oak trees grow.

Bears, moose, beavers, and white-tailed deer live in Maine. The streams are filled with trout and salmon, and many other kinds of fish and sea creatures swim in the coastal waters. The bald eagle soars above Maine's rivers and woodlands.

Maine is known for the dense fog that rolls in during the early mornings.

Winters are very cold in northern Maine, with heavy snowfall and temperatures that plunge below zero. Along the coast, the climate is warmer in the winter and cooler in the summer than it is in the interior. Fog often rolls in from the ocean.

The state gets plenty of rain each year. Storms called **northeasters** whip in from the ocean, creating huge waves.

Home of the Abenaki

Humans have lived on the North American continent since the time when ice covered the area that later became Maine. These people and their descendants are called Indians, or Native Americans. After the glaciers melted, bands of people entered the region that became Maine. The major group in Maine was the Abenaki. *Abenaki* means "people of the dawnland."

The Abenaki lived off the natural bounty of the land. In the spring they fished for salmon, bass, and sturgeon in streams and rivers. In the summer they gathered nuts, such as acorns, and picked many kinds of berries. They caught shellfish in the ocean. In the fall they hunted deer, moose, beavers, and bears.

Maine has fascinated people for centuries with its natural beauty *(left)*. Maine's wilderness holds an abundance for berry pickers *(right)*.

Hunting and Gathering

What did the Native Americans eat? The answer is simple: everything they could. They gathered a wide variety of plants and nuts and hunted many kinds of animals. At one archaeological site in the northeastern United States, remains of all these foods were found.

great auk

beaver	sturgeon	bald eagle
dog	sea bass	great auk
red fox	wolf fish	loon
mink	bay scallop	great blue heron
deer	mussel	mallard
harbor seal	long clam	red-tailed hawk
snapping turtle	moon snail	
stingray	thick-lipped dill	

Using birchbark, the Abenaki built canoes, which they used for traveling and fishing in lakes and rivers. They made snowshoes to make walking and hunting easier in the winter snow.

Source: *The Smithsonian Book of North American Indians: Before the Coming of the Europeans* by Phillip Kopper.

This wigwam, built in the early 1900s, is similar to those used by the Abenaki.

The Abenaki lived in cone-shaped **wigwams** made of animal hides or birch bark. Tribes moved from place to place to find the best food and game. Older Abenaki family members passed down stories and legends to young people, who were taught to respect the land and animals. The Abenaki's way of life lasted for hundreds of years, until white people came to the area.

Many Europeans were inspired to set sail for the "New World" after Christopher Columbus's voyage to the Caribbean islands in 1492. Some of these explorers reached the coast of Maine.

Around A.D. 1000, Vikings from Scandinavia sailed to the northeastern coast of North America. After Christopher Columbus's voyage to the Americas in 1492, many Europeans set off for this "New World."

One explorer who reached the northeast was John Cabot, who worked for the king of England. England then claimed ownership of the land that Cabot had discovered.

Throughout the 1500s, English, Spanish, Italian, and French explorers ventured along the coast of Maine and into the interior. They reported on the natural riches they found—trees, fish, animals, and water.

In 1604 two Frenchmen established a **colony** of about 70 people on an island near what later became the border of Maine. After a freezing winter with few supplies, the French settlers returned to France.

British captain George Waymouth was the next European to explore Maine's coast. In 1605 he kidnapped five Abenaki Indians and took them back to Britain with him. Two men who worked for Britain's King James I—Sir Ferdinando Gorges and Sir John Popham—questioned the Indians about their home. Using a few English words and lots of gestures, the Abenaki described their beautiful lands.

French explorer Samuel de Champlain established a colony near the border of modern-day Maine.

Convinced that this faraway territory could prove valuable, Gorges and Popham decided to sponsor a settlement there. In 1607 Popham's nephew, George Popham, brought a group of settlers to the mouth of the Kennebec River to build the colony that his uncle wanted. The settlement lasted only a year, however. The settlers lost their leaders when George Popham and John Popham died in 1607.

A few years later, the French returned to the northeast. They settled on Mount Desert Island in 1613, but a British captain drove them off the island. He declared that the island belonged to Britain.

During the next decades, both the French and the British staked out sections of North America for their colonies. The

In the 1800s, this fort was built on the original site of the first British settlement on Popham Beach.

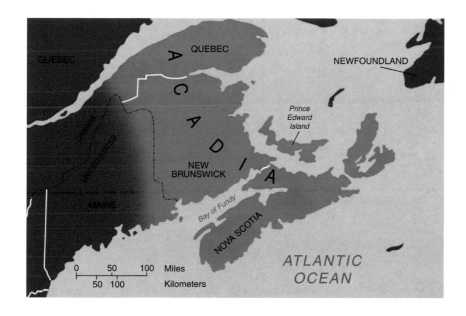

Eastern Maine and parts of eastern Canada made up the French colony of Acadia.

French claimed part of what became eastern Maine. This land, along with territory in eastern Canada, made up the French colony of Acadia.

In 1622 King James I of Britain gave Ferdinando Gorges and John Mason land in Maine. The British built several small settlements in Maine during the 1620s and 1630s. The white settlers carried diseases that were new to the Indians. Smallpox wiped out many Abenaki. In some places, three out of every four people died.

The Abenaki tried to keep the British from taking over the land the Indians had lived on for generations. The Indians and British fought often, and many people were killed in bloody battles. The Indians got along better with the French, who traded European goods to the Abenaki for furs.

After Ferdinando Gorges died in 1647, the British-owned Massachusetts Bay Colony claimed Maine as part of its territory. In 1691 Maine became part of Massachusetts.

This 1755 conflict between Native Americans and British soldiers was one of many deadly battles during the French and Indian War.

The British fought the French for control of land in New England on and off from 1689 to 1763. The Abenaki usually sided with the French in these battles. The last conflict, called the French and Indian War, began in 1754. France lost, and the **treaty,** signed in 1763, gave Britain control of most of North America. Many Abenaki fled to Canada. Only a small number of Indians remained in Maine.

Between 1690 and 1760, the white population of Maine increased tenfold. The new settlers, like the Indians before them, made use of the natural resources in the area. The land offered plenty of wood to use for timber and shipbuilding. The colonists built elegant wooden sailing ships and sold them to other colonies. The settlers also fished in the coastal waters.

Early settlers found Maine's abundant trees to be a valuable resource.

THE TOWN of FALMOUTH, *Burnt by Captain MOET, Oct.*

A British attack destroyed most of the town of Falmouth during the Revolutionary War, as shown in this 1791 drawing.

In 1775 Maine became involved in the American War of Independence. In June, Maine patriots captured a British ship, and the first naval battle of the Revolution was fought at Machias, Maine. Later the same year, British troops bombarded the city of Falmouth (later renamed Portland), Maine, with heated cannonballs. Three-fourths of the town burned.

After the war ended in 1783, Maine's population continued to grow by leaps and bounds. The Massachusetts government sold land in Maine to settlers for less than a dollar an acre. Many people from Massachusetts and New Hampshire moved to Maine. Between 1783 and 1791, the population of Maine increased by 40,000.

In 1820 Maine separated from Massachusetts and became the 23rd state. Maine entered the United States as part of the Missouri Compromise. This compromise was an agreement in Congress to keep the number of states with slaves equal to the number of states without slaves. Since Missouri was a territory where slavery was allowed, it was not granted statehood until after Maine entered the Union as a free state.

The new state of Maine seemed to have a promising future. Its vast wilderness marked a frontier full of possibility.

This sketch shows what life was like at an early Maine settlement.

Mainers continued to rely on shipbuilding and lumber to make a living. Each year from December through May, lumberjacks lived in Maine's forests. They cut pine logs, hauled them by sled, and piled them next to the Kennebec and Penobscot Rivers.

In March or April, during "ice out," the ice on the river broke up. Lumberjacks threw the logs into the

Horses pull a sleigh of lumber. The lumber industry has provided Mainers with jobs for more than three centuries.

river, and the river current carried them downstream to sawmills near the seaports. Maine sold a lot of lumber to other states.

A Yarmouth shoe factory in 1910. Leather and textile factories opened in Maine in the mid-1800s.

In the mid-1800s, textile (cloth) and leather factories opened throughout New England, including Maine. Lumbering and fishing, however, remained the state's best money-makers.

A new industry sprang up in the late 1800s— paper. Between 1868 and 1900, paper mills opened in several towns in Maine, such as Mechanic Falls, Westbrook, and Yarmouth. Many paper mills used rivers for **hydropower**—a cheap form of electricity —to run their machines.

Thousands of French Canadians crossed the border to find jobs in Maine's textile mills. Soon a large community of French Americans lived in Maine. **Immigrants** from other countries, such as Ireland, came to the state, too.

As white people settled on more territory, the original inhabitants of Maine—the Indians—lost almost all of their land. By the 1850s, most Indians lived on just a couple of **reservations,** areas of land set aside for them.

The U.S. government forced Abenaki Indians to give up their land and live on reservations by the mid-1800s. Many Abenaki continue to live on this land.

Maine began to be known as an ideal vacation spot in the early 1900s.

Throughout the mid- to late 1800s, many farmers left Maine and moved west, where the land was better for farming. This trend continued into the 1900s. After the invention of the steamboat, demand for sailing ships fell. This hurt Maine's shipbuilding industry.

By 1900 people from other states were beginning to discover some of the mystique of Maine—its unspoiled beauty and lack of crowded cities. Maine Central Railroad opened a ticket office in New York City and ran newspaper advertisements encouraging New Yorkers to visit Maine.

While the tourism industry grew, some industries declined during the early 1900s. Many small farms shut down. The state lost many textile mills when they were moved to the southern states, where cloth could be produced more cheaply. But Maine continued to make more and more paper products. Conditions for Maine's workers got worse during the Great Depression, a period of hard times for the whole country.

The invention of the steamship greatly reduced the need for sailboats produced in Maine.

But Maine's economy recovered during World War II (1939–1945). Thousands of Mainers served in the U.S. military. Others worked in the state's shipyards, where hundreds of ships were built for the U.S. Navy. Some Mainers who worked in mills made shoes and uniforms for soldiers.

After World War II, tourists continued to flock to Maine's forests, mountains, and beaches. To accommodate them, Mainers expanded the highway system, opened ski resorts, and built motels.

Maine's fishing activities, such as digging for clams, became less common in the 1900s.

Although tourists brought a lot of money into the state, many Mainers faced hard times in the mid-1900s. Maine never had much heavy industry.

This helped keep the state clean and the population low, but it also meant that for many Mainers, finding a job was tough. The traditional activities—lumbering, fishing, and farming—did not provide enough jobs for everyone who wanted a job.

Although logging is still an important industry, the majority of Mainers hold service jobs.

President Jimmy Carter signs the Maine Indian Claims Settlement Act in 1980. This law gave Maine's Native Americans money both to buy land and to save for future generations.

In 1972 the Passamaquoddy, Penobscot, and Maliseet Indians asked the U.S. government to give back land they felt had been illegally taken from them during the late 1700s and 1800s. In 1980 a court ruled that the U.S. government should pay the Indians more than $81 million for the land. The Indians used the money to buy some of their land back from the government.

In the 1980s and 1990s, Maine's economy improved in some ways. New service jobs were created in businesses such as retail stores, restaurants, and government. Land along the coast increased in value. New homes, offices, and factories were built. By the end of the 1980s, a large number of jobs were in the state's largest city, Portland. But economic problems remained in northern and central Maine. Jobs in industries such as fishing and manufacturing continued to decline. After a century of hardship, Mainers take pride in their state's natural beauty and look to the future for better times.

PEOPLE & ECONOMY

Logging, Lobsters, and Leisure

ompared to most other states, the number of people who live in Maine is small—just over one million. In the northern part of the state in particular, towns are few and far between. In Maine you can get away from busy cities and crowds of people. This is part of Maine's mystique.

Residents of Maine's small towns enjoy the state's open spaces.

Almost half of Maine's 1,275,000 residents live in urban areas. Most people live along the coast. The state's largest city is Portland, with about 64,000 people. Other large communities include Lewiston, Bangor, and Augusta, the capital.

Most Mainers live along the Atlantic coast *(opposite page)*. The state's largest city is Portland *(below)*.

Maine's residents find many ways to work and play. A lobster festival is held in Rockland each summer.

Almost all Mainers were born in the United States. Their ancestors came mostly from Britain, France, and Canada. In some towns near the Canadian border, many residents still speak French.

Maine has small numbers of African Americans, Latinos, and Asian Americans. Together, these groups make up about 2 percent of the state's population.

About 7,000 Native Americans live in Maine. The two major groups, the Penobscot and the Passamaquoddy, are descendants of the original Abenaki.

Jobs in hospitals are one kind of service. Here a dietary aide prepares a meal at Maine Medical Center in Portland.

Most Mainers—63 percent—work in jobs that provide a service. Service businesses include stores, motels, restaurants, schools, and hospitals. About 14 percent of workers have jobs in government. Altogether, these activities account for about 76 percent of the money that people in the state make each year.

Another big part of Maine's economy is manufacturing—the making of goods. Paper products earn more money than any other good manufactured in the state. Paper companies make newsprint for newspapers and glossy paper for magazines, as well as facial tissues and paper towels.

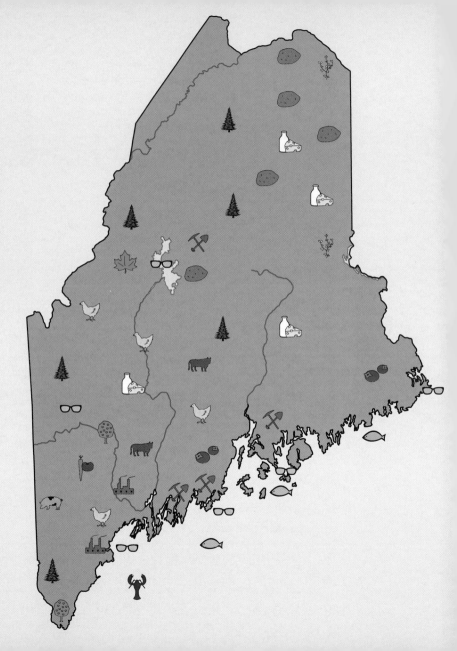

MAINE
Economic Map

The symbols on this map show where different economic activities take place in Maine. The legend below explains what each symbol stands for.

	Beef cattle		Manufacturing
	Blueberries		Maple syrup
	Dairy products		Oats
	Fish		Potatoes
	Forest products		Poultry
	Fruit		Stone
	Hogs		Tourism
	Lobster		Vegetables

Potato farmers in Aroostook County use machines to harvest and haul their valuable crop.

Many Mainers work in the forest-products industry. They cut down trees, haul logs, and make wood products. Besides lumber and paper, some wood items made in Maine include matches, toys, and furniture. Maine makes more toothpicks than any other state.

Although farming is not a large part of Maine's economy, some farm products are important. Dairy farms dot the countryside. Potatoes—grown in the rich soil of the Aroostook Plateau—are the state's most valuable farm crop. Maine's potato output is one of the highest in the nation. More blueberries are grown in Maine than in any other state in the country. Apples are Maine's most valuable fruit crop.

A Few Facts about Lobsters

The lobster is a crustacean. Crustaceans are animals that have hard shells and no backbones. The lobster's hard shell covers its body like a suit of armor. Lobsters' shells are dark green or blue, and they turn red when they're cooked. Lobsters have two large claws that extend out in front, four pairs of legs for walking, and a tail that spreads out like a fan.

Lobsters live on the bottom of the ocean near shore. They hide in holes or under rocks. The lobster fisher traps lobsters in cages called pots, which are lowered to the ocean floor. Fish are placed in the pots as bait. The lobster can walk into the trap but can't find its way out. The fisher hauls the traps up from the bottom of the sea with a strong cord that connects the trap to a buoy that floats on the surface of the water.

The pots are left in the water for a day or two. Then the fisher hauls up the traps, removes the catch, adds new bait, and returns the pots to the bottom. People who make their living from fishing for lobster use anywhere from 400 to 1,000 traps.

An average Maine lobster weighs about 1.5 pounds, but some deepwater lobsters weigh as much as 20 pounds.

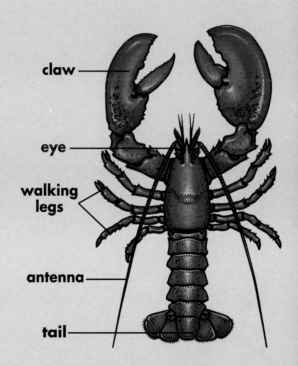

claw

eye

walking legs

antenna

tail

46

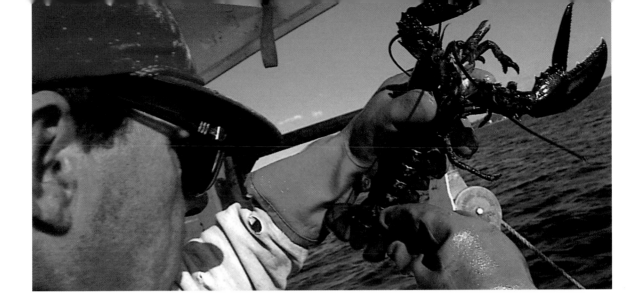

Maine is famous for its lobsters. Lobster boats and lobster shacks are a common sight along the coast. Lobster fishers haul in about 47 million pounds of lobster each year. Clams, cod, flounder, and other fish and shellfish add to Maine's annual seafood harvest.

Factories in Maine freeze or can foods to be sold throughout the country. The state's farmers send apples, potatoes, and blueberries to factories where they are made into juice, french fries, and other foods. Workers at plants package chicken and can sardines and other seafood.

Before deciding whether to keep his catch, a lobster fisher checks to see if it is a female. Female lobsters are thrown back so that they can lay eggs and produce more lobsters.

Tourism provides many jobs for Mainers. Each year, millions of people travel to Maine, where they discover what makes the state special. Acadia National Park on Mount Desert Island draws many visitors.

Tourists also flock to the coast, with its white lighthouses and salty air, or they head north to the forests, lakes, and mountains. Many people visit the woods in autumn, when the leaves burst into a brilliant display of yellow, red, and orange.

Maine's historic lighthouses *(right)* and peaceful lakes *(opposite page)* are a couple of the state's most popular tourism sites.

In many towns in Maine, you can visit a historical building or a museum. Mainers host a variety of special events, such as the Houlton Potato Feast and the Maine Lobster Festival. Near Moosehead Lake, 100 teams compete in a dogsledding race each winter.

There are plenty of things to do and see in Maine. Some activities include *(left to right)* "spud wrestling" in mashed potatoes at the Potato Festival in Fort Fairfield, sailing, cross-country skiing, and folk dancing at the New Sweden Historical Museum.

For nature lovers, Maine offers plenty to do. You can hike, camp, fish, sail, swim, bicycle, or go rock climbing in the summer. In the winter, Mainers and tourists enjoy downhill and cross-country skiing, ice skating, snow-mobiling, and ice fishing.

Many plants and animals, including these harbor seals, live along Maine's coast.

THE ENVIRONMENT

Coast Guarding

or Mainers, the state's beautiful seashores, forests, lakes, and rivers provide a sense of identity and pride as well as a source of money and jobs. For visitors, Maine is a place to enjoy the wilderness and the clean waterways. But like other states, Maine faces threats to its environment.

One environmental issue for Maine is to keep its shores and coastal waters clean. The coast is home to many kinds of birds, plants, animals, and fish. Many people earn money by fishing in the ocean. Tourists and residents alike appreciate the scenery along the coast.

Acadia National Park in
Bar Harbor, Maine

Maine's oceanfront
beaches are crowded
with buildings
and people.

More and more people are moving to Maine's
southern coast. Even though the coast is only
a small part of all the land in Maine, almost
two-thirds of the state's people live and work there.

The growth in population has led to a lot of development, or building. Some of this development interferes with the environment.

For example, the risk of water pollution increases. Water pollution comes from several sources. Sometimes, the source is obvious, such as tankers that spill oil or factories that dump waste into the sea.

Other times, however, the source of pollution is not as clear. Some everyday activities can also pollute the ocean. Pollutants such as lawn and garden fertilizers, animal wastes, and salts used on icy roads wash into drains and eventually into the ocean.

More and more businesses and homes are being built along Maine's southern coast.

Litter and household wastes can also pollute water. Fish get tangled in plastic bags and containers. Birds eat small pieces of plastic. Some scientists say that the plastic yokes that hold six-packs of soda pop will last for 400 years!

When many houses are built along a stretch of Maine's coast, some animals lose their natural habitat. Some species, such as the bird called the puffin, are in danger of extinction—they may not exist in the future.

Maine continues to take steps to protect its shores and to keep its water from becoming more polluted. Each year during Coastweek, more than 1,000 volunteers pick up trash along the coast. In 1999 these citizens collected more than 12,000 pounds of trash from 289 miles of shoreline. Various organizations help people who own land along Maine's coast

If Maine's coast becomes too overcrowded, the puffin could lose its home.

Maine's beaches are home to unique plants such as beach peas.

to keep the water clean. The state government has passed laws against dumping waste into the ocean. Other laws determine how coastal land can be used. For example, new factories or homes can be built in some areas, but the state has set aside other land especially for wildlife.

This painted rock is a reminder to all who live in and visit Maine to do their part in keeping it clean.

All of Maine's citizens can help out by picking up litter along the coast, by recycling trash, and by learning how to cut down on activities that cause pollution. Mainers know that their natural resources are valuable. Everyone can work together to protect the environment and to keep Maine beautiful.

Mainers such as these volunteers help keep the state free of litter.

ALL ABOUT MAINE

Fun Facts

Northern Maine is a good place to spot a moose. Maine has more moose than any other state besides Alaska. You're most likely to see moose at dawn or dusk. They hide among the trees, and they stand in shallow lakes and streams eating water plants.

The L. L. Bean outdoor goods store in Freeport, Maine, is the state's second biggest tourist attraction. Every year about 2.5 million people visit the store, which features an indoor trout pond.

Portland Head Light may be the most photographed lighthouse in the United States. Each year, more than 350,000 people visit the lighthouse at the entrance to Portland's harbor. Most of them take pictures of it. Portland Head Light is also the oldest of Maine's more than 65 lighthouses. It has guided ships safely along the rocky coast since 1791.

Most of the lobsters eaten in the United States come from Maine. The world's largest lobster boiler is in Rockland, Maine. The boiler is 24 feet long and can steam 5,000 pounds of lobster in an hour.

George H. W. Bush, the 41st president of the United States, makes his summer home in the seaside town of Kennebunkport, Maine.

December 17 is Chester Greenwood Day in Maine. Greenwood invented earmuffs in Farmington, Maine, in 1873. He made the ear protectors out of beaver fur, wire, and cloth. Greenwood, who also invented a folding bed and a wide-bottom kettle, started a successful earmuff factory in Farmington.

STATE SONG

In 1931 Maine officials held a contest to select a state song. "State of Maine Song," written by Roger Vinton Snow, was chosen from among 115 submissions. Also known as "O Pine Tree State," the song was adopted as the official state song in 1937.

STATE OF MAINE SONG

Words and music by Roger Vinton Snow

You can hear "State of Maine Song" by visiting this website:

<http://www.50states.com/songs/maine.htm>

A MAINE RECIPE

Maine is an important producer of wild blueberries. Every August, thousands of people come to Union, Maine, for the annual Wild Blueberry Festival. There, they celebrate blueberries by eating them in every way imaginable. One classic way to eat blueberries is in muffins, which you can make with this recipe.

BLUEBERRY MUFFINS

You will need:

1 cup blueberries
2 cups flour
½ cup sugar
1 tablespoon baking powder

½ teaspoon salt
1 egg, beaten
¼ cup melted butter
1 cup milk or buttermilk

1. Have an adult preheat the oven to 375° F. Grease the cups of a 12-muffin pan.
2. Gently toss blueberries with ¼ cup flour in a bowl.
3. Mix the rest of the flour with sugar, baking powder, and salt in a large bowl.
4. Using a mixer or by hand, stir in egg, butter, milk, and blueberries.
5. Fill each cup of the muffin pan about two-thirds full of batter.
6. With an adult's help, bake 20 to 25 minutes. Cool for 5 minutes before removing the muffins from the pan.

HISTORICAL TIMELINE

5000 B.C. The first humans arrive in Maine.

A.D. 1000 Vikings reach the northeast coast of North America.

1500 Explorer John Cabot sails along Maine's coast.

1604 French explorer Samuel de Champlain establishes a colony on the Saint Croix River.

1607 The Popham colony, the first settlement in Maine, is established.

1613 French settlers live on Mount Desert Island.

1622 King Charles I divides land between John Mason and Ferdinando Gorges. Gorges's share becomes the province of Maine.

1691 Maine becomes part of the Massachusetts Bay Colony.

1754 Mainers begin fighting in the French and Indian War (1755–1763).

1775 The American Revolutionary War (1775–1783) begins. The first naval battle of the war occurs near Machias in Maine.

1820   Maine becomes the 23rd state to join the Union.

1900   Tourism takes hold as a big business in Maine.

1939   World War II (1939–1945) begins. Maine's shipyards are busy making ships for the war.

1972   A group of Native Americans sues the U.S. government over land in Maine that was unfairly taken from them.

1980   The Maine Indian Claims Act awards land and money to Maine's Native Americans.

1983   Eleven-year-old Samantha Smith, from Manchester, Maine, writes a peace-making letter to Soviet leader Yuri Andropov. On his invitation, she visits the Soviet Union.

1991   The Maine state government shuts down during a budget crisis.

1997   William Cohen of Bangor is appointed secretary of defense under President Clinton.

1998   Senator George Mitchell of Maine works to make peace in Northern Ireland.

OUTSTANDING MAINERS

L. L. Bean

Leon Leonwood (L. L.) Bean (1873–1967), born near Bethel, Maine, founded the nationally known L. L. Bean company, which sells outdoor clothing and gear through catalogs and stores. The flagship store is in Freeport, Maine.

Milton Bradley (1836–1911), born in Vienna, Maine, was a pioneer in the game business. In 1864 he founded the Milton Bradley Company, which makes popular board games such as Life, Chutes and Ladders, and Candyland.

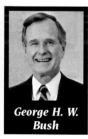

Milton Bradley

George Herbert Walker Bush (born 1924), a summer resident of Kennebunkport, Maine, served as the 41st president of the United States from 1989 to 1993. Bush also served as a U.S. congressman, as ambassador to the United Nations (UN), as director of the Central Intelligence Agency (CIA), and as vice president under Ronald Reagan.

George H. W. Bush

William Sebastian Cohen (born 1940) was born and raised in Bangor, Maine. Cohen got his start in politics by serving as a Bangor city council member and later as Bangor's mayor. He was elected to the House of Representatives in 1972 and to the U.S. Senate in 1978. President Bill Clinton appointed Cohen as secretary of defense in 1997.

Dorothea Dix (1802–1887) was a teacher and social reformer who was born in Hampden. While teaching prisoners, she observed the terrible conditions under which mentally ill prisoners lived. Dix helped open special hospitals for the mentally ill in the United States and Canada. She also served as a nurse in the Civil War.

William Cohen

John Ford (1894–1973) grew up in Cape Elizabeth and headed to Hollywood as a young man. He was a famous director of western movies, including *Stagecoach, How the West Was Won,* and *The Quiet Man.* Ford won six Academy Awards for his movies, which featured stars like John Wayne, Henry Fonda, and Maureen O'Hara.

John Ford

Hannibal Hamlin (1809–1891) was born in Paris Hill, Maine. Hamlin was vice president of the United States from 1861 to 1865, during Abraham Lincoln's first term. Hamlin strongly opposed slavery.

Winslow Homer (1836–1910) was a painter celebrated for his powerful seascapes and portrayals of everyday heroes. Two of his most famous paintings are *The Gulf Stream* and *The Fog Warning.* Homer made his home in Prout's Neck, Maine.

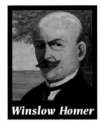

Winslow Homer

Stephen King (born 1947), who is from Bangor, Maine, is a novelist. King has written many popular horror novels, including *Apt Pupil, The Green Mile, The Shining,* and *Cujo.*

Stephen King

Henry Wadsworth Longfellow (1807–1882), born in Portland, Maine, was the most famous American poet of the 1800s. His works include *Evangeline, The Song of Hiawatha,* and *The Courtship of Miles Standish.* He is also remembered as the author of the famous poem "Paul Revere's Ride."

John Marin (1870–1953) was one of the first American artists to paint in a modern style. His watercolor and oil paintings capture the windblown seascapes and landscapes of Maine. He died in Addison, Maine.

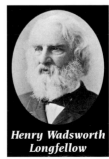

Henry Wadsworth Longfellow

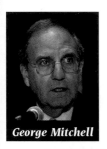

George Mitchell

Edmund Muskie

Joan Benoit Samuelson

Margaret Chase Smith

Edna St. Vincent Millay (1892–1950) was a writer who was born in Rockland, Maine. Millay was the first American woman to win the Pulitzer Prize for poetry. She is known for the book *The Ballad of the Harp-Weaver* and an opera called *The King's Henchman.*

George Mitchell (born 1933) represented Maine in the U.S. Senate from 1980 until 1995. From 1989 until 1995 the Democrat served as the Senate Majority Leader. He is known for his efforts to make peace in Northern Ireland. Mitchell is from Waterville.

Edmund Muskie (1914–1996) came from Rumford, Maine. Muskie ran for vice president of the United States in 1968 (along with Hubert Humphrey as presidential candidate), but they lost the race. Muskie was the first Democrat from Maine to serve in the U.S. Congress.

Edwin Arlington Robinson (1869–1935), born in Head Tide, Maine, was a poet. Among his books of poetry are *The Man Who Died Twice* and *Tristram.*

Joan Benoit Samuelson (born 1957) grew up in Cape Elizabeth, Maine. A runner, Benoit won the Boston Marathon in 1979 and 1982 and a gold medal for the marathon in the 1984 Summer Olympics. She also won the America's Marathon in 1985.

Margaret Chase Smith (1897–1995) grew up in Skowhegan, Maine. She was the first woman elected to both houses of the U.S. Congress. Smith was a member of the House of Representatives before she served in the Senate from 1949 to 1973.

Samantha Smith (1972–1985) was born in Houlton, Maine. When she was 10 years old, she wrote a letter to Soviet leader Yuri Andropov and visited the U.S.S.R. as his guest. She later died in a plane crash.

Samantha Smith

Louis Sockalexis (1871–1913), born in Old Town, Maine, played professional baseball for the Cleveland Spiders from 1897 to 1899. The team was later renamed the Cleveland Indians in honor of Sockalexis, a Penobscot Indian.

Louis Sockalexis

Percy LeBaron Spencer (1894–1970), born in Howland, Maine, invented the microwave oven in 1946. The first microwave oven weighed 750 pounds and was almost six feet high!

E. B. White (1899–1985), an author and humorist, wrote the children's literature classics *Charlotte's Web*, *Stuart Little*, and *Trumpet of the Swan*. White was awarded the Laura Ingalls Wilder Medal in 1970 and received the National Medal for Literature in 1971. He was a staff writer for the *New Yorker* magazine for many years. White spent much of his life on his farm in Allen Cove, Maine.

E. B. White

Andrew Wyeth (born 1917) is an artist who spends summers in Cushing, Maine. Wyeth's paintings often depict people and places in rural Maine. He was awarded the Congressional Gold Medal in 1990.

Andrew Wyeth

FACTS-AT-A-GLANCE

Nickname: Pine Tree State

Song: "State of Maine Song"

Motto: Dirigo (I Direct)

Flower: white pine cone and tassel

Tree: white pine

Bird: chickadee

Animal: moose

Fish: landlocked salmon

Insect: honeybee

Fossil: *pertica quadrifaria*

Date and ranking of statehood:
    March 15, 1820, the 23rd state

Capital: Augusta

Area: 30,865 square miles

Rank in area, nationwide: 40th

Average January temperature: 15° F

Average July temperature: 67° F

The state flag of Maine bears
the state seal.

POPULATION GROWTH

Millions

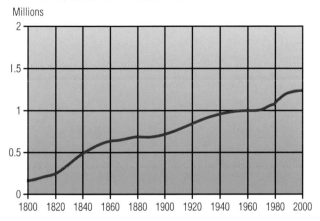

This chart shows how Maine's population has grown from 1800 to 2000.

The state seal of Maine was adopted in 1820. It shows a farmer, a seaman, a pine tree, and a moose. The North Star at the top of the seal represents Maine's northern location.

Population: 1,274,923 (2000 census)

Rank in population, nationwide: 40th

Major cities and populations: (2000 census) Portland (64,249), Lewiston (35,690), Bangor (31,473), South Portland (23,324), Auburn (23,203), Brunswick (21,172)

U.S. senators: 2

U.S. representatives: 2

Electoral votes: 4

Natural resources: fertile soil, forests, garnet, granite, limestone, stone

Agricultural products: apples, beef cattle, blueberries, eggs, hay, milk, potatoes, poultry

Fishing industry: clams, cod, flounder, lobster, ocean perch, pollock, sea herring

Manufactured goods: clothing, electrical machinery and equipment, food products, leather products, lumber and wood products, paper products, rubber and plastic products, textiles, transportation equipment

WHERE MAINERS WORK

Services—63 percent (services includes jobs in trade; community, social, and personal services; finance, insurance, and real estate; transportation, communication, and utilities)

Government—14 percent

Manufacturing—13 percent

Construction—6 percent

Agriculture—4 percent

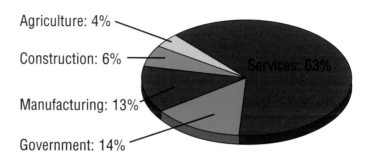

Agriculture: 4%
Construction: 6%
Manufacturing: 13%
Government: 14%
Services: 63%

GROSS STATE PRODUCT

Services—63 percent

Manufacturing—17 percent

Government—13 percent

Construction—5 percent

Agriculture—2 percent

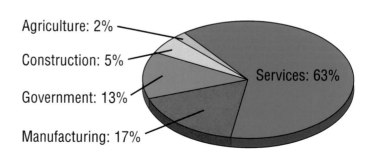

Agriculture: 2%
Construction: 5%
Government: 13%
Manufacturing: 17%
Services: 63%

Finback whales

MAINE WILDLIFE

Mammals: black bear, bobcat, eastern cougar, finback whale, fox, humpback whale, lynx, Maine coon cat, mink, moose, raccoon, white-tailed deer

Birds: bald eagle, chickadee, grasshopper sparrow, least tern, owl, peregrine falcon, piping plover, sedge wren

Fish: alewife, Atlantic salmon, brook trout, cod, flounder, hake, landlocked salmon, mackerel, pickerel, pollock, smallmouth bass, striped bass, tuna, white and yellow perch

Amphibians and reptiles: box turtle, leatherback turtle

Trees: balsam fir, basswood, beech, hemlock, maple, oak, spruce, white pine, yellow and white birch

Wild plants: American stickweed, alpine azalea, bushy aster, chestnut oak, Dragon's mouth, flatleaf willow, furbish lousewort, green spleenwort, Jacob's ladder, small whorled pogonia, water stargrass, wild indigo

PLACES TO VISIT

Acadia National Park
Located on the rocky shore of Mount Desert Island, the park's geography ranges from meadows and marshes to dense evergreen forests. The natural beauty provides many opportunities for outdoor fun such as hiking, backpacking, and camping.

Old Fort Western, Augusta
Built in 1754, this is the oldest surviving wooden fort in the United States. Visitors can tour the museum, watch military exercises, and see what life was like in the 1700s.

Acadia National Park

Old Gaol Museum, York

The oldest public building in Maine, built in 1653, served as a jail until 1860. Once housing dangerous criminals, the former jail became York's first museum. The jail's cells and jailkeepers' quarters still appear as they might have in the 1700s.

Penobscot Marine Museum, Searsport

The museum's vast display of valuable paintings, ship models, old sailing charts, navigation instruments, fishing and whaling equipment, and other items provide a link to marine history.

Portland Head Light, near Portland

Built in 1791, this lighthouse is one of the oldest and most famous American lighthouses. It towers 101 feet over the surf.

Seashore Trolley Museum, near Kennebunkport

Having 250 antique trolley and transit vehicles, this is the largest museum of historic electric railroad equipment in the United States. Museum visitors climb on board a restored trolley and travel through Maine's countryside, over part of the old Atlantic Shore interurban trolley line.

Shore Village Museum, Rockland

The largest collection of lighthouse artifacts in the United States is showcased in this museum. Exhibits include buoys, life-saving gear, ship models, and carvings made from whale teeth, whalebone, and sea shells.

Wadsworth-Longfellow House/Maine History Gallery, Portland

The boyhood home of poet Henry Wadsworth Longfellow ranks as Maine's most popular historic site.

ANNUAL EVENTS

International Snowmobilers Festival, Madawaska—*February*

MooseStompers Weekend, Houlton—*February*

Caribou Winter Carnival and Snowmobile Festival—*February*

Clam Festival, Yarmouth—*July*

Crown of Maine Balloon Festival, Caribou—*July*

Potato Blossom Festival, Fort Fairfield—*July*

World's Fastest Lobster Boat Races, Jonesport—*July*

Windjammer Days, Boothbay Harbor—*July*

Blueberry Festival, Union—*August*

Lobster Festival, Rockland—*August*

Maine Festival of the Arts, Portland—*August*

Northern Maine Fair, Presque Isle—*August*

Maine State Fair, Lewiston—*September*

LEARN MORE ABOUT MAINE

BOOKS

General

Aylesworth, Thomas G. *Northern New England: Maine, New Hampshire, Vermont.* New York: Chelsea House, 1991.

Fradin, Dennis B. *Maine.* Chicago: Children's Press, 1994.

Kent, Deborah. *Maine.* Danbury, CT: Children's Press, 1999. For older readers.

Special Interest

Beneduce, Ann Keay. *A Weekend with Winslow Homer.* New York: Rizzoli International Publications, Inc., 1993. Winslow Homer invites readers into his Maine home and shares details of his life and of his accomplishments as an artist.

Collins, David R. *To the Point: A Story about E. B. White.* Minneapolis: Lerner Publications Company, 1989. Collins tells the story of the author of *Charlotte's Web*, whose writing is beloved by generations of readers and writers.

Kress, Stephen W. *Project Puffin: How We Brought Puffins Back to Egg Rock.* Gardiner, ME: Tilbury House, 1997. Details a wildlife scientist's successful efforts to restore puffin colonies in Maine.

Quasha, Jennifer. *Maine Coon Cats.* New York: The Rosen Publishing Group, Inc., 2000. Learn about physical features and origins of Maine's hearty, hairy state cat.

Fiction

Field, Rachel. *Calico Bush.* New York: Simon & Schuster, 1998. For older readers. First published in 1931, this Newbery Honor Book tells the story of Marguerite, a French girl who comes to Maine during the 1700s. Marguerite is "bound-out" to a family that she must serve for six years.

Hopkinson, Deborah. *Birdie's Lighthouse.* New York: Atheneum, 1997. The diary of a 10-year-old girl who moves with her family in 1855 from a town in Maine to rugged Turtle Island when her father gets a job as the lighthouse keeper.

MacLachlan, Patricia. *Skylark.* New York: HarperCollins, 1994. After surviving hardships on a prairie farm, a mother takes her children to her childhood home on the coast of Maine.

Woodruff, Elvira. *The Ghost of Lizard Light.* New York: Alfred A. Knopf, Inc., 1999. Fourth-grader Jack Newton and his family move into an old lighthouse keeper's lodge, right on the edge of the Atlantic Ocean, where he meets a mysterious young boy.

WEBSITES

The State of Maine
<http://www.state.me.us/>
Maine's official website includes government news, information about living and working in Maine, and a kids' page.

Official Maine State Tourism Website
<http://www.visitmaine.com>
Visit this website for up-to-date information about Maine's attractions, activities and events, facts about Maine, and local links.

The Maine Resource Guide
<http://www.maineguide.com>
This website provides plenty of information about the best places to visit while in Maine, dates of upcoming events, and other helpful facts.

Bangor Daily News
<http://www.bangornews.com>
Read about Maine's current events in the online version of the state's largest daily newspaper.

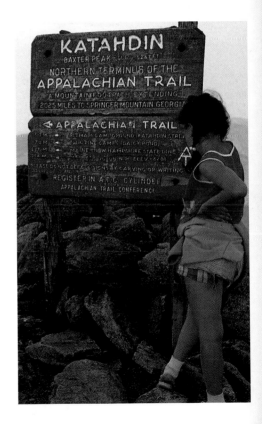

PRONUNCIATION GUIDE

Abenaki (ab-uh-NAH-kee)

Acadia (uh-KAY-dee-uh)

Aroostook (uh-ROOS-tuhk)

Androscoggin (an-druh-SKAWG-uhn)

Houlton (HOHLT-uhn)

Katahdin (kuh-TAWD-uhn)

Kennebec (kehn-uh-BEHK)

Kennebunkport (kehn-uh-BUHNK-port)

Machias (muh-CHEYE-uhs)

Passamaquoddy (PAS-uh-muh-
KWAWD-ee)

Penobscot (puh-NAWB-skuht)

GLOSSARY

colony: a territory ruled by a country some distance away

glacier: a large body of ice and snow that moves slowly over land

hydropower: the electricity produced by using waterpower; also called hydroelectric power

ice age: a period when ice sheets covered large regions of the earth. The term Ice Age usually refers to the most recent one, called the Pleistocene, which ended about 12,000 years ago.

immigrant: a person who moves to a foreign country and settles there

northeaster: a strong storm or wind that blows in from the northeast

reservation: public land set aside by the government to be used by Native Americans

treaty: an agreement between two or more groups, usually having to do with peace or trade

wigwam: a kind of tent used by some Native Americans, shaped in a dome or cone and covered with bark, grass-woven mats, leaves, or other material

INDEX

PHOTO ACKNOWLEDGMENTS

Cover photographs by © Buddy Mays/CORBIS (left) and © Judy Griesedieck/ CORBIS (right); Digital Cartographics, pp. 1, 8, 9, 44; © Kevin Fleming/CORBIS, pp. 2-3; © Wolfgang Kaehler/CORBIS, p. 3; Michael J. Kilpatrick, pp. 4 (detail), 7 (detail), 17 (detail), 39 (detail), 53 (detail); Voscar, The Maine Photographer, pp. 6, 10, 11, 12, 39, 40, 41, 42, 45, 48, 49, 50 (left), 51 (right); © James P. Rowan, pp. 7, 53, 74; Paul A. Knaut, Jr., p. 13; Maine Office of Tourism, p. 14 (bottom); Maine Coast Heritage Trust, pp. 14 (top), 54, 55; Brian Kent, p. 15; Alan J. LaVallee, pp. 16, 17; Kevin Shields, p. 18; Lia E. Munson/Root Resources, p. 19; Laura Westlund, pp. 20, 25, 46, 70 (bottom); The University Museum, University of Pennsylvania (Neg. #S4-139082), p. 21; Independent Picture Service, p. 22; Library of Congress, pp. 23, 26; Collections of the Maine Historical Society, pp. 24, 28, 30, 34, 35, 36, 67 (second from top and bottom); Kitty Kahout/Root Resources, pp. 27, 79; Maine State Museum, p. 31; Collection of the Yarmouth (Maine) Historical Society, p. 32; Peabody Museum, Harvard University/Photograph by Hillel Burger, p. 33; © Howard Ande, p. 37; Jimmy Carter Library, p. 38; Audiovisual Resource Department, Maine Medical Center, p. 43; John Alphonse, p. 47; Chewonki Foundation, Wiscasset, Maine, p. 50 (right); Kim T. Fenn, pp. 51 (left), 80; Gold Thread Photography, pp. 52, 59; Benjamin Goldstein/Root Resources, p. 56; Michelle E. Noel, p. 57; Stan Osolinski/Root Resources, p. 60; Jack Lindstrom, p. 61; Tim Seeley, 63, 71, 72 (both); Bernard Carpenter photo, L.L. Bean, Inc., p. 66 (top); Milton Bradley Company, p. 66 (second from top); David Valdez, The White House, p. 66 (second from bottom); © AFP/CORBIS, pp. 66 (bottom), 68 (top); © Hulton-Deutsch Collection/CORBIS, p. 67 (top); © John-Marshall Mantel/CORBIS, p. 67 (second from bottom); Maine Democratic Party, p. 68 (second from top); Duomo/Steven E. Sutton, p. 68 (second from bottom); United States Senate Historical Office, p. 68 (bottom); TASS/Sovfoto, p. 69 (top); National Baseball Library, Cooperstown, N.Y., p. 69 (second from top); Donald E. Johnson, p. 69 (second from bottom); © Oscar White/CORBIS, p. 69 (bottom); Jean Matheny, p. 70 (top); © Judy Griesedieck/CORBIS, p. 73.